A Closer Look at Plants

STEM

Alicia Klepeis

Rourke
Educational Media

rourkeeducationalmedia.com

Before Reading:

Building Academic Vocabulary and Background Knowledge

Before reading a book, it is important to tap into what your child or students already know about the topic. This will help them develop their vocabulary, increase their reading comprehension, and make connections across the curriculum.

1. *Look at the cover of the book. What will this book be about?*
2. *What do you already know about the topic?*
3. *Let's study the Table of Contents. What will you learn about in the book's chapters?*
4. *What would you like to learn about this topic? Do you think you might learn about it from this book? Why or why not?*
5. *Use a reading journal to write about your knowledge of this topic. Record what you already know about the topic and what you hope to learn about the topic.*
6. *Read the book.*
7. *In your reading journal, record what you learned about the topic and your response to the book.*
8. *After reading the book complete the activities below.*

Content Area Vocabulary
Read the list. What do these words mean?

glucose
herbaceous
node
nutrients
phloem
seedling
tubers
wilt
xylem

After Reading:

Comprehension and Extension Activity

After reading the book, work on the following questions with your child or students in order to check their level of reading comprehension and content mastery.

1. *What are the main tasks that stems do for plants?* (Summarize)
2. *Could plants survive without stems?* (Infer)
3. *How are woody stems different from herbaceous stems?* (Asking questions)
4. *Have you eaten any edible plant stems? Which ones?* (Text to self connection)
5. *What are some reasons that plant stems might wilt or droop?* (Asking questions)

Extension Activity

After reading the book, try this activity. You'll need two glasses or jars. Add a small amount of water to one jar but leave the other one empty (dry). Into each jar, place one twig, one rose (with its stem), and one flower like a tulip or dandelion (also with its stem). Leave these stems in the jars for a couple of days. What are the differences between the stems in the dry jar and those in the water-filled jar?

Table of Contents

Rourke 20.95 12/1/18

duckweed

sequoia tree

Plants Are Everywhere

Picture a potted plant in a windowsill. Or an elm tree in your backyard. Plants are all around us. Plants come in many sizes, shapes, and colors. Huge sequoia trees are hundreds of feet tall. But duckweed plants are as tiny as ice cream sprinkles!

Plants of all sizes usually have the same main parts, including roots, a stem, and leaves.

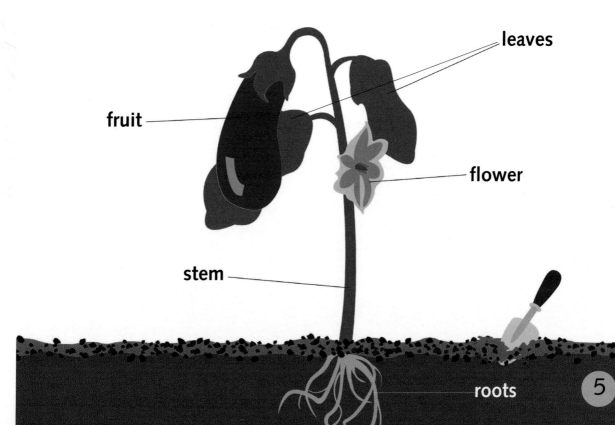

leaves

fruit

flower

stem

roots

How Plants Grow

Most plants grow from seeds. Each seed contains a tiny plant inside. What do seeds need to grow? They need water and sunlight. They also need a good location.

If a seed has these things, it will grow into a
seedling. Its roots will grow into the ground.
But its stem will grow towards the sun.

Supporting a Plant

A plant's stem helps it to grow and survive. It does this in many ways. One important job of the stem is to support the plant. The stem is like your backbone. Without it, you would flop over. You couldn't stand straight.

Have you ever seen a plant stem tip over? That can happen if the plant is not getting enough light. Plants can also droop for other reasons. Without enough water moving through its stem, a plant can **wilt**.

The plant on the left looks healthy. The one on the right is drooping and losing its leaves, perhaps because it needs more water.

Staking A Plant

Sometimes plant stems need a little extra support. Why? They may bend from the weight of fruit or flowers. Take a tomato plant, for example. Gardeners often add a wooden stake and tie some string loosely around the stem. This helps keep the plant upright.

Reaching for the Sun

Plants grow toward the sun. Why? They need sunlight to live. Plants use sunlight to help them make food.

The stem allows the plant to reach for the light. Have you ever seen indoor flowers leaning toward a window? Their green stems grow and bend toward the sun. An ivy plant's stem twists and curls to get sunlight too.

All of the sunflowers in this field are reaching up to face the sun.

Water and Nutrients

All plants need water and **nutrients** to grow big and strong. Calcium and nitrogen are two examples. People also need certain vitamins and minerals to be healthy.

A plant's stem is connected to the roots and leaves. The **node** is the part of the stem from which a leaf or branch grows. A plant can have many nodes.

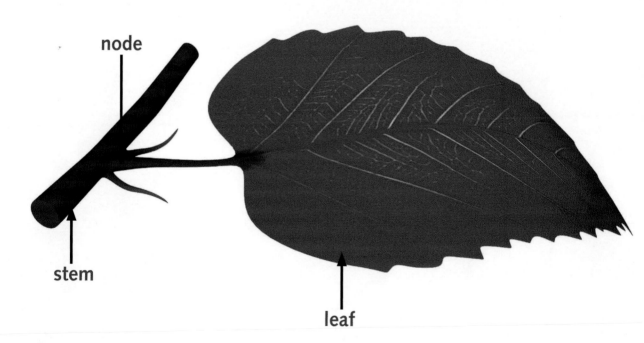

node

stem

leaf

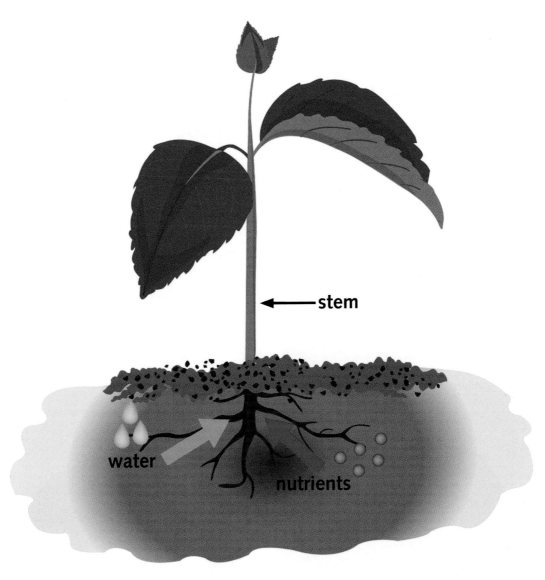

stem

water

nutrients

First the plant's roots absorb water and nutrients from the soil. Then the stem takes over. It passes these items to the rest of the plant. The stem brings water and nutrients to the leaves.

How do water, minerals, and food travel through the stem? A stem has special tubes inside it. These tubes are called **xylem** and **phloem**. These tubes have different jobs. Xylem transports water and dissolved minerals from the roots to the leaves.

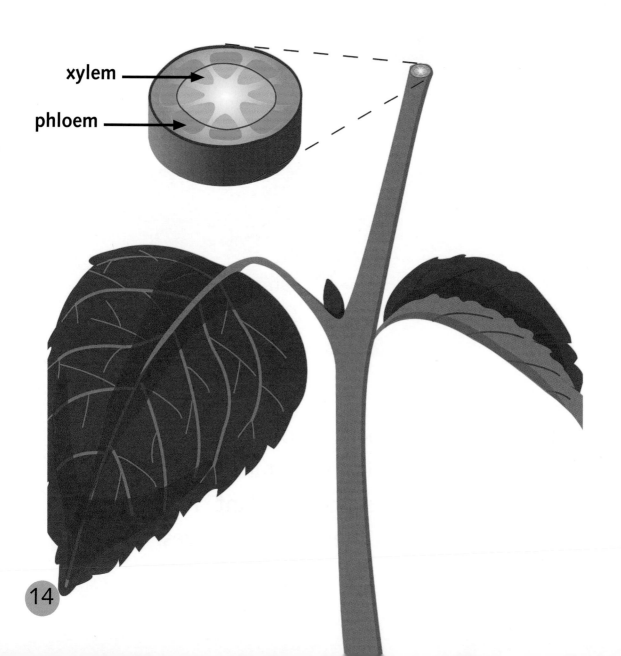

xylem

phloem

Phloem moves food from a plant's leaves to the rest of the plant. This is not food like pizza or hamburgers. Plants make their own kind of food. They make it in their leaves. This food is a sugar called **glucose**. It gives the plant energy to thrive.

The stem is like a highway transporting water and food throughout a plant.

Stems That We Eat

People around the world eat plant stems. Sounds wacky, right? Asparagus is a stem. So are celery and rhubarb. Potatoes are actually edible storage stems called **tubers**. Stems can be tasty! So the next time you help cook something, try some edible plant stems!

Stems for Storage

Stems support plants. They also provide a transportation system for nutrients and water. But some stems can also store food. The stems of sugarcane and potatoes store food that plants can use later. This stored food can help plants grow.

Baobab Trees

Baobab trees are commonly found in dry areas of Africa and Australia. These amazing trees are like sponges. They store water in their woody stems. This helps these trees survive through seasonal droughts. How much water can a baobab store? Tens of thousands of gallons!

Ever wonder how cactus plants survive in the desert? Cactus stems store water. This allows the plants to live through long dry periods.

Canary Island spurge cactus

Types of Stems

Do all plant stems look the same?
No. Some plants have woody stems. The trunk of
a tree is actually its stem. Woody stems are strong.
They support a plant well. These stems do not
bend. They are brittle.

Not all plants have woody stems. Some stems are soft. Lots of flowers have soft, or **herbaceous**, stems. So do many houseplants. These stems are more delicate. They bend.

How Does Water Travel Through A Plant's Stem?

Let's find out!

What You'll Need:

- a glass
- water
- ruler
- teaspoon
- red or blue food coloring
- a piece of celery with the leaves attached
- a knife
- a piece of paper and pen

What You'll Do:

1. Pour about 2 inches (5 centimeters) of water into a glass.

2. Add 2 teaspoons (9.86 milliliters) of food coloring to your glass of water. Stir well.

3. Have an adult cut off the bottom inch (2.5 centimeters) from the celery stalk.

4. Place the cut end of the stalk into the glass full of colored water.

5. On your piece of paper, make a prediction about what you think will happen to the celery.

6. Leave the celery overnight in the colored water.

7. The next day, write down what you observed. Was your prediction right?

Glossary

glucose (GLOO-kose): a naturally produced sugar in plants which is a source of energy for living things

herbaceous (huhr-BAY-shuhs): referring to a stem with little or no woody tissue

node (nohd): the part of the stem from which a leaf or branch grows

nutrients (NOO-tree-unhts): substances such as minerals or vitamins that are needed by people, animals, or plants to stay healthy and strong

phloem (FLOW-em): a tissue in plants containing tubes that carry sugars downward from the leaves through the plant

seedling (SEED-ling): a young plant which has been grown from a seed rather than a cutting

tubers (TOO-buhrs): thickened underground parts of a stem that serve as a food reserve

wilt (wilt): to lose freshness and become limp; to droop

xylem (ZI-luhm): a tissue in plants that carries water and dissolved nutrients upward from the root through the plant

Index

Show What You Know

1. Why are stems important to plants?
2. What are the two main types of stems and how are they different?
3. In which direction do stems tend to grow?
4. What is the difference between xylem and phloem?
5. How might people use plant stems?

Websites to Visit

www.bbc.co.uk/schools/gcsebitesize/science/add_ocr_gateway/green_world/planttransportrev1.shtml

http://easyscienceforkids.com/plant-parts-facts-for-kids-video/

http://ny.pbslearningmedia.org/resource/5dea21b4-6c92-46ff-982c-8650f9429c01/think-garden-plant-structure/

About The Author

Meet The Author!
www.meetREMauthors.com

From circus science to jellybeans, Alicia Klepeis loves to research fun and out-of-the-ordinary topics that make nonfiction exciting for readers. Alicia began her career at the National Geographic Society. She is the author of numerous children's books, including *Bizarre Things We've Called Medicine* and *The World's Strangest Foods*. She does not have a green thumb but has managed to keep one cactus alive for over 20 years. Alicia lives with her family in upstate New York.

www.rourkeeducationalmedia.com

PHOTO CREDITS: Cover: background photo © bamboo background © life-literacy, stem diagram cross-section © udaix. plant © Jakinnboaz; page 4-5 plant diagram © Jakinnboaz, sequoias © My Good Images, duckweed © Magnetic Mcc; page 6-7 seed growing © showcake, sun © ZaZa Studio; page 8 upright flower © jannoon028, drooping flowers © akiyoko, page 9 © vvoe; page 10-11 © RM911; page 12-13 leaf.node diagram © sciencepics, page 13 and 14 © Jakinnboaz, page 15 © benjamas11; page 16-17 cactus © underworld, baobab tree © Raffaella Fiore; page 18-19 © Arthur Linnik; page 20 © LittleMiss. All photos images Shutterstock.com

Edited by: Keli Sipperley

Cover and Interior design by: Nicola Stratford   www.nicolastratford.com

Library of Congress PCN Data

Stem/ Alicia Klepeis
  (A Closer Look at Plants)
   ISBN 978-1-68342-385-0 (hard cover)
   ISBN 978-1-68342-455-0 (soft cover)
   ISBN 978-1-68342-551-9 (e-Book)
Library of Congress Control Number: 2017931265

Rourke Educational Media
Printed in the United States of America, North Mankato, Minnesota